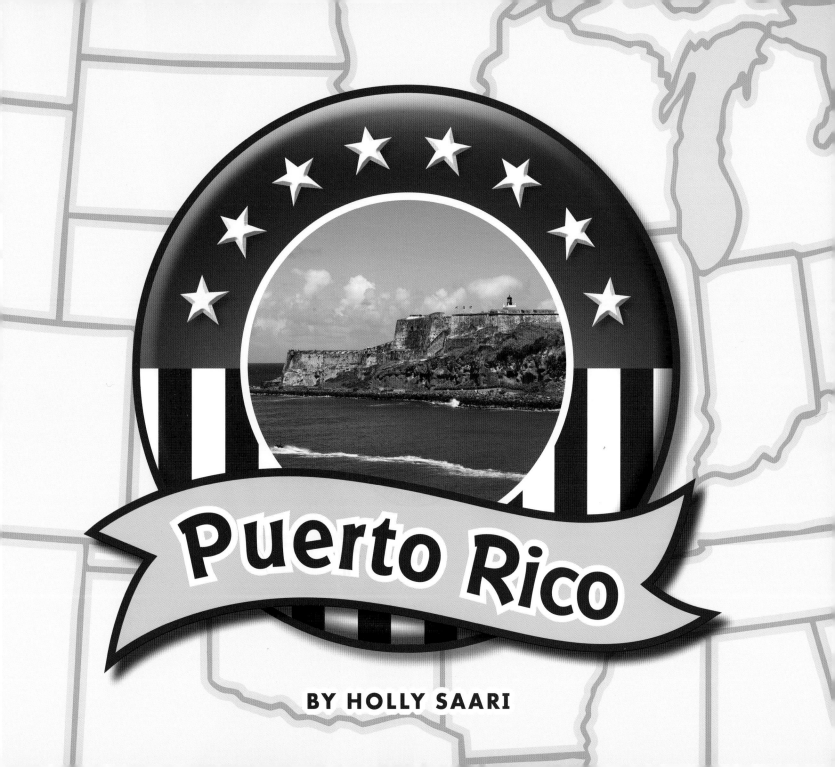

Puerto Rico

BY HOLLY SAARI

The Child's World

Published by The Child's World®
1980 Lookout Drive • Mankato, MN 56003-1705
800-599-READ • www.childsworld.com

ACKNOWLEDGMENTS
The Child's World®: Mary Berendes, Publishing Director
The Design Lab: Design and production
Red Line Editorial: Editorial direction

PHOTO CREDITS: Robert Young/iStockphoto, cover, 1, 3; Matt Kania/Map
Hero, Inc., 4, 5; Lawrence Sawyer/iStockphoto, 7; Nick Tzolov/iStockphoto,
9; SpectrumPhotofile, 10; Joe Ferrer/Shutterstock Images, 11; Ewing
Galloway/Photolibrary, 13; iStockphoto, 15; Pat Canova/Photolibrary, 17;
Stephen Chernin/AP Images, 19; Shutterstock Images, 21; One Mile Up, 22;
Quarter-dollar coin image from the United States Mint, 22

LIBRARY OF CONGRESS CATALOGING-IN-PUBLICATION DATA
Saari, Holly.
 Puerto Rico / by Holly Saari.
   p. cm.
 Includes bibliographical references and index.
 ISBN 978-1-60253-483-4 (library bound : alk. paper)
 1. Puerto Rico—Juvenile literature. I. Title.

F1958.3.S23 2010
972.95—dc22

2010019322

Printed in the United States of America in Mankato, Minnesota.
July 2010
F11538

On the cover:
El Morro is a
fortress in Puerto
Rico that was built
in the 1500s.

CONTENTS

Geography

Let's explore Puerto Rico! Puerto Rico is an island in the Caribbean Sea. It is southeast of Florida and north of South America. Puerto Rico is a **Commonwealth** of the United States. The United States rules it, but Puerto Rico also has its own government.

Atlantic Ocean

Barceloneta

San Juan

Arecibo

Bayamón

Manatí

Carolina

San Sebastián

Fajardo

Culebra Island

Mayagüez

PUERTO RICO

Mona Island

San Germán

Vieques Island

Juana Díaz

Guánica

Ponce

Maunabo

Puerto Rico means "rich port" in Spanish.

Caribbean Sea

NORTH
EAST
SOUTH
WEST

Cities

San Juan is the capital of Puerto Rico. It is the largest city on the island. Bayamón is another large city. Both are in the north. Ponce is a city in the south. It is known for its art.

San Juan was founded in 1521. ▶

Land

There are many mountains on the island of Puerto Rico. There are **plains**, too. The island has several rivers. Puerto Rico has beaches along its coastline.

Waterfalls are part of Puerto Rico's natural beauty. ▶

Plants and Animals

A large part of Puerto Rico is a **rain forest**. Many tropical plants grow here. There are coconut trees, too. The island has many birds. The **official** bird is the stripe-headed tanager. The southwest part of the island does not have many trees. It does not rain much there.

Many different types of trees, ferns, and flowers grow in El Yunque National Forest. ▶

11

People and Work

About 4 million people live in Puerto Rico. Many of them work in **tourism**. **Manufacturing** is a large business in Puerto Rico. Factories on the island make clothes, medicine, and food.

Some Puerto Ricans work as farmers. Sugarcane and coffee are grown on the island. ▶

History

Christopher Columbus landed on Puerto Rico in 1493. Many native peoples lived on the island when he arrived. Spain ruled the island for many years. The United States took control of it on December 10, 1898.

Spanish and English are the official languages in Puerto Rico.

A statue in San Juan honors Christopher Columbus. ▶

Ways of Life

Puerto Rico has many types of music and art. The people have many **traditions**. These have been shaped by Spain, the United States, Africa, and the Caribbean islands.

Dancing is one Puerto Rican tradition. ▶

Famous People

Singer Ricky Martin was born in Puerto Rico. He sings pop music. Roberto Clemente played in Major League Baseball. He was from Puerto Rico. Julia de Burgos was a well-known poet from Puerto Rico.

Ricky Martin was born in San Juan. ▶

Famous Places

Puerto Rico is known for its many beaches. People travel year-round to visit them. Old San Juan is a **popular** place. It has very old buildings. They show the history of the island.

Structures built in the 1500s and 1600s ▶ still stand in Old San Juan.

Symbols

Seal

The *F* and *I* on Puerto Rico's seal stand for Ferdinand and Isabella. They ruled Spain when Puerto Rico was discovered. The lamb lying down stands for peace. Go to childsworld.com/links for a link to Puerto Rico's Web site, where you can get a firsthand look at the seal.

Flag

Puerto Rico's flag was first used in 1895. The white star stands for the Commonwealth of Puerto Rico. The white stripes stand for rights and freedom.

Quarter

Puerto Rico's quarter shows stone walls used to guard San Juan. The quarter came out in 2009.

Glossary

Commonwealth (KOM-un-welth): A Commonwealth is land with its own government that is united with and ruled by another country. Puerto Rico is a Commonwealth of the United States.

manufacturing (man-yuh-FAK-chur-ing): Manufacturing is the task of making items with machines. Many people work in manufacturing jobs in Puerto Rico.

official (uh-FISH-ul): Official means approved by a government or an authority. Puerto Rico's official bird is the stripe-headed tanager.

plains (PLAYNZ): Plains are areas of flat land that do not have many trees. Part of Puerto Rico has plains.

popular (POP-yuh-lur): To be popular is to be enjoyed by many people. San Juan is a popular place in Puerto Rico.

rain forest (RAYN FOR-ist): A rain forest is a wooded area with high yearly rainfall. Part of Puerto Rico is a rain forest.

seal (SEEL): A seal is a symbol a state or Commonwealth uses for government business. Puerto Rico has a seal that shows a lamb lying down.

symbols (SIM-bulz): Symbols are pictures or things that stand for something else. The seal and the flag are Puerto Rico's symbols.

tourism (TOOR-ih-zum): Tourism is visiting another place (such as a state or country) for fun or the jobs that help these visitors. Tourism creates many jobs in Puerto Rico.

traditions (truh-DISH-unz): Traditions are a specific people's beliefs and ways of life. Puerto Rico has traditions from many countries.

Further Information

Books

Keller, Laurie. *The Scrambled States of America*. New York: Henry Holt, 2002.

Reynolds, Jeff. *A to Z: Puerto Rico*. New York: Children's Press, 2004.

Thornton, Brian. *The Everything Kids' States Book: Wind Your Way Across Our Great Nation*. Avon, MA: Adams Media, 2007.

Web Sites

Visit our Web site for links about Puerto Rico: *childsworld.com/links*

Note to Parents, Teachers, and Librarians: We routinely verify our Web links to make sure they are safe and active sites. So encourage your readers to check them out!

Index